CAFE DE COSTA RICA TOKENS

Errol Rojas

Print information available on the last page

Rev. date: 08/09/2019

To order additional copies of this book, contact:
Xlibris
1-888-795-4274
www.Xlibris.com
Orders@Xlibris.com

Catalog of Café de Costa Rica Tokens

The purpose of this guide is to demonstrate and catalog the most common Costa Rican coffee farm tokens, known in Costa Rica as *boletos*. Although they are the most common, it has become a daunting challenge for me the author to fully complete and document this particular series. The majority of these tokens are easily identified by the following legends: Café de Costa Rica, Café, Ferretería EL IRIS, and ALMACEN GAMBOA. These tokens are stock pieces which were more economical to use and widely available; therefore, the small farm owner simply stamped a combination of initials, numbers, or symbols on one or both faces. On the other hand, wealthy estate owners were able to have private die-struck tokens made with their names as part of the token legend. For example, CRISANTO BENEVIDES and DORA ZAMORA CH, just to name a couple. You will notice these examples, and others, throughout the catalog.

I have listed the tokens in an alphabetic, visual, and narrative manner. If the immediate goal is to determine who the farm owner is, or where it is located, then this catalog will help you narrow your search. With four parts to choose from, you can quickly find the right spot for your coffee token. Understandably, some of the tokens illustrated in this catalog are part of a series of other Costa Rican die-struck tokens. What will become apparent, as you turn the pages and view the tokens, is that there are subtle varieties, sizes, and creativeness. Letters were either incuse or raised, and there are small dots and big dots. Presumably, the dots were placed in order to divide the legends. What's noticeable throughout this series is that not all tokens have these dots. I have identified the ones that do. You will also notice whole numbers and half numbers were counterstamped or raised to assign a denomination. The most common denominations used were 1/4, 1/2, 1, and 5. Farm owners also became ingenious and started adding symbols to the tokens; unfortunately, their individual meanings were lost overtime. The symbols sometimes resemble things we know; on others, they must have been used in an allegorical fashion. Lastly, Costa Rican farm owners started identifying their tokens with engravings. The process of artistically engraving is rarely seen on other Latin American tokens.

Occasionally, farm owners utilized someone else's tokens by acquiring their farm and their respective tokens. The new owner either obliterated the previous stamping or added bigger or smaller stampings to the tokens to singularly identify it was his to the employees. Having done this made it difficult for the collector to know which stamp came first, but it shows a relationship that can be studied in-depth by historians. I know from a collector's point of view that it is harder to complete into one's collection all of the varieties that may exist for a particular coffee farm. Most coffee farm owners continued to stamp and engrave new tokens when the old ones were badly worn or lost.

The tokens listed in this catalog were used as currency to pay the employees for picking bushels of ripe coffee beans. In Spanish, this is called *canastos de café*. When the coffee pickers worked a whole day, they would take the *canastos de café* and deliver them to the receiver. The receiver, otherwise known in Spanish as a *recibidor*, would count the bushels at the end of the day and pay the picker accordingly. The bushels may have contained full or partial amounts of ripe beans which accounted for the different denominations on the tokens. The tokens accrued were used as daily wages. Customarily, at the end of the work week, the workers would convert the tokens for official currency from the farm owner. Some tokens do not have an assigned denomination, and only the farm owner and the workers at the time knew that a small-size token meant one denomination while a bigger one meant another. Wealthy estate owners had their own commissary on the farm, and the employee could use the tokens as a form of money to buy provisions. It is understood that a large percentage of coffee pickers at the turn of the twentieth century lived and worked on the farms.

The bushels the workers used for the coffee beans were made of willow twigs known in Spanish as *mimbre*. *Mimbre* is largely available throughout the country, and the workers weaved their own baskets for collecting coffee. When the coffee beans were prepared for export, they were placed inside burlap bags which had the name of the owner or farm stenciled on the outside. The burlap bags were then transported with oxcarts to the processing plant.

I am cognizant that this is not the definitive collection—for which I apologize—but no one really knows how many Café de Costa Rica tokens and varieties exist in the market, or when they first appeared. Some stock tokens have been identified by other authors like Russell Rulau, Jerry Schimmel, Hector Rojas Solano, and Elisa Carazo de Flores. What sets this catalog apart from previous authors is the sole dedication to Café de Costa Rica tokens and their varieties. All of which played a large part in Costa Rican culture and prosperity.

This collection has been several years in the making, both the accumulating and documenting. Not included in this collection are photos and descriptions of Café de Costa Rica tokens owned by other collectors. My goal in the writing of this catalog is to emphasize what collectors seem to overlook— the most common of the Costa Rican coffee tokens. Even in Costa Rica, most collectors neither pay attention nor actively seek this sort of token. The only reason some people collect these tokens is because it completes a particular farm owner's series. I place a value on all tokens from Costa Rica and will continue to collect and document them. I trust this catalog will bring focus and study to this growing series of tokens.

While some of the tokens shown in the following pages are easy to obtain, others, of course, are not. Unfortunately, throughout the twentieth century in Costa Rica, it became common practice to either destroy or throw tokens away. In some rare instances, people hoarded them. Ever since Costa Rica produced more official coinage, there became a decreasing need in minting stock coffee tokens. According to author and collector Russell Rulau, the hobby of collecting and selling Costa Rican tokens has been around since the 1980s or earlier. Thus, throughout the Americas, the challenging hobby of collecting tokens (known as *exonumia*) has begun to flourish. Though collecting tokens from Europe and North America existed decades before coffee tokens came to form, I derive a great sense of satisfaction from the fact that coffee tokens have been added to the discriminating collector's list.

Collecting tokens will sometimes lead you to the question, should I clean this token or not? A challenging decision this may be as I, too, have asked myself the very same question. Collectors have the greatest difficulties with grimy and hard-to-read tokens. Though I suspect a true purist would never clean a coin or a token, my personal recommendation would be if you must clean a very dirty token, use a soft toothbrush with mild soap and water. Then, dry it with a sponge or cotton cloth.

Throughout this catalog, you will note some tokens have abundant background information given in order to better identify tokens, including their locations and owners—on others there is none. This information in large part has been researched by other authors, dealers, and collectors. I shall continue visiting coin shows and consulting with individual dealers and fellow collectors within Costa Rica and the United States for updated token information. I trust readers, fellow collectors, and/or dealers will assist me in updating this catalog in order to correct possible mistakes and help fill in gaps. So please, take your time and compare my catalog with your collection and note varieties and/or scarcities. I look forward to hearing from you.

Contents

<u>Acknowledgement</u>

In this section, I would like to give honorable mentions of merit to people instrumental in helping me with my quest and thirst for collecting Costa Rican tokens. First, I would thank God and my family for giving me strength and patience. In the beginning, I recall starting with a handful of tokens which included part of this collection and almost leaving it at that. Once I was invited to attend a coin show in San José, Costa Rica, and that's where I saw how big this hobby really was. There are collectors from all walks of life and from all over the world all looking for the same thing—a new coin, new paper money, or tokens. Focusing on what appears, at least to me, as the most challenging aspect in Costa Rican *exonumia*, I have collected and cataloged as many Café de Costa Rica tokens and varieties as possible. During this journey, I most enjoyed the wonderful collectors and dealers I met along the way who provided me with their invaluable time and information on conditions and rarities. My special appreciation to them appears below in alphabetical order.

Manuel Ayala – Hails from Connecticut and really got me started into collecting tokens in a large way and gave me direction and ideas. If Manuel had never contacted me, it is true that I would not be writing this catalog today.

José Angel Rojas Chaverri – Is from San Rafael de Heredia and has been collecting since he was seven years old. José has the largest token collection in all of Costa Rica, and I am amazed by his exclusive tokens of ex-presidents. I enjoyed seeing his token collection and trading with him.

Rodolfo Fernández Duarte – I met him at a local coin show. Besides having the same things in common like coin and token collecting, he has taken the time out to invite my family to his home. He shared his exclusive collection with me and has provided information to quench my thirst of where some of these tokens originated in Costa Rica.

Elisa Carazo de Flores – A published author in San José on Costa Rican coffee tokens, she provided me with a wealth of information and shared her very valuable time with me. We also enjoy trading tokens. I am awed by her two-thousand-plus Costa Rican token collection.

Minor Martín – Has aided me in providing new material and trades. He owns a store named Filatelia y Numismática La Granada in San José, Costa Rica.

Mauricio Soto – I am pleased with the contacts Mauricio has provided me. With his help, I have been able to track down dealers and collectors in San José.

Bibliography

Costa Rica Tokens. Jerry F. Schimmel Copyright 1984 San Francisco, California

Latin American Tokens 2nd Edition. Russell Rulau Copyright 2000 Krause Publications, Iola, Wisconsin

Los boletos de café en Costa Rica: folleto técnico. Por Manuel Chacon Hidalgo y Elisa Carazo de Flores. 1.a ed San José C.R., Fundación Museos Banco Central de
Costa Rica, 2002

<u>Café de Costa Rica</u>

This section has the largest amount of stock coffee tokens which will assist you in noting varieties, sizes, and denominations. I list these first in the catalog since they are the most abundant. The peculiarity that exists here, which does not exist anywhere else in this catalog, is that some token legends were made with lowercase letters versus the norm in uppercase.

CCR 1   AB, J M Arce Bartolini
    Location: Lagunilla, Heredia
    Obverse: Café de Costa Rica
    Reverse: Initials AB
    Size: 21.9 mm
    Metal: Brass

CCR 2   AB, J M Arce Bartolini
    Location: Lagunilla, Heredia
    Obverse: Café de Costa Rica
    Reverse: Initials AB
    Size: Octagonal 20.7 mm
    Metal: Copper

CCR 3   AC, Angela Coronado, Family of Rodríguez Pérez
    Location: Belén, Heredia
    Obverse: Café de Costa Rica
    Reverse: Initials AC
    Size: 21.9 mm
    Metal: Brass

CCR 4   AC, Angela Coronado, Family of Rodríguez Pérez
    Location: Belén, Heredia
    Obverse: Café de Costa Rica
    Reverse: Initials AC
    Size: 24 mm
    Metal: Zinc Coated

CCR 5   ACO
    Location:
    Obverse: CAFÉ DE COSTA RICA, Initials ACO, Dot
    Reverse: Denomination 1
    Size: 25.8 mm
    Metal: Brass

CCR 6   AE, Arturo Echandi
  Location: Cartago
  Obverse: Café de Costa Rica, Initials SR (San Rafael de Calderón Guardia), Initial I
  Reverse: Initials AE
  Size: 21.9 mm
  Metal: Brass

CCR 7   AGA, Adelo García Alvarado
  Location: Santo Domingo, Heredia
  Obverse: CAFÉ DE COSTA RICA, Initial 0, Denomination 1
  Reverse: Initials AGA
  Size: 27 mm
  Metal: Brass

CCR 8   AMB, Ana María Barquero
    Location: Santo Domingo, Heredia
    Obverse: CAFÉ DE COSTA RICA, Denomination 1
    Reverse: Initials AMB
    Size: 27 mm
    Metal: Brass

CCR 9   Allegorical Symbol
    Location:
    Obverse: CAFÉ DE COSTA RICA, Denomination 1
    Reverse: Allegorical Symbol
    Size: 27 mm
    Metal: Brass

CCR 10   AP, Alfonso Peralta
    Location: Cartago
    Obverse: Café de Costa Rica, Initials AP
    Reverse: Blank
    Size: 21.9 mm
    Metal: Brass

CCR 11   AR, Adela Rodríguez Pérez
    Location: Heredia
    Obverse: Café de Costa Rica, Initials AR
    Reverse: Blank
    Size: 24 mm
    Metal: Zinc Coated

CCR 12   AV, Aurelia Villalobos
    Location: Santo Domingo, Heredia
    Obverse: CAFÉ DE COSTA RICA, Denomination 1
    Reverse: Initials AV
    Size: 27 mm
    Metal: Brass

CCR 13   Basic Design
    Location:
    Obverse: Café de Costa Rica
    Reverse: Blank
    Size: 21.9 mm
    Metal: Zinc Coated

CCR 14   Basic Design
    Location:
    Obverse: CAFÉ DE COSTA RICA, Denomination ½
    Reverse: Blank
    Size: 22.7 mm
    Metal: Brass

CCR 15   Basic Design
    Location:
    Obverse: CAFÉ DE COSTA RICA, Denomination 1
    Reverse: Blank
    Size: 27 mm
    Metal: Brass

CCR 16   Basic Design
    Location:
    Obverse: CAFÉ DE COSTA RICA, Denomination 5
    Reverse: Blank
    Size: 31.7 mm
    Metal: Brass

CCR 17   BR, Bidal Rodríguez
    Location: Heredia
    Obverse: CAFÉ DE COSTA RICA, Denomination 1, Initials BR
    Reverse: Blank
    Size: 27 mm
    Metal: Brass

CCR 18   BSR, Beneficio San Rafael
    Location: Puriscal
    Obverse: CAFE DE COSTA RICA Denomination ¼
    Reverse: Initials BSR
    Size: 19 mm
    Metal Brass

CCR 19   BSR, Beneficio San Rafael
    Location: Puriscal
    Obverse: CAFE DE COSTA RICA Denomination ½
    Reverse: Initials BSR
    Size:
    Metal Brass

CCR 20   BVB, Benigno Viquez Barrantes
    Location: Getsomaní, San Rafael Heredia
    Obverse: CAFÉ DE COSTA RICA, Denomination 1
    Reverse: Initials BVB
    Size: 27 mm
    Metal: Brass

CCR 21   C, Angela Coronado, Family of Rodríguez Pérez, see CCR 3
    Location: Belén, Heredia
    Obverse: Café de Costa Rica
    Reverse: Initial C
    Size: 21.9 mm
    Metal: Brass

CCR 22   CA
    Location:
    Obverse: Café de Costa Rica, Initials CA
    Reverse: Blank
    Size: 24 mm
    Metal: Zinc Coated

CCR 23   CB
    Location: Aserrí
    Obverse: Café de Costa Rica, Initials CB
    Reverse: Initials MMF, María Mercedes Fallas
    Size: 24 mm
    Metal: Zinc Coated

CCR 24   Coffee Bean
    Location:
    Obverse: CAFÉ DE COSTA RICA, Dot
    Reverse: Denomination ½, Stamped Coffee Bean
    Size: 23.7 mm
    Metal: Brass

CCR 25   Coffee Bean
    Location:
    Obverse: CAFÉ DE COSTA RICA, Dot
    Reverse: Denomination 1, Stamped Coffee Bean
    Size: 26 mm
    Metal: Brass

CCR 26   Crisanto Benevides Hernández
     Location: Heredia
     Obverse: CAFÉ DE COSTA RICA, Dot
     Reverse: CRISANTO BENEVIDES H, Denomination ¼, Dot
     Size: 20.5 mm
     Metal: Brass

CCR 27   Crisanto Benevides Hernández
     Location: Heredia
     Obverse: CAFÉ DE COSTA RICA, Dot
     Reverse: CRISANTO BENEVIDES H, Denomination ½, Dot
     Size: 22.5 mm
     Metal: Brass

CCR 28   Crisanto Benevides Hernández
     Location: Heredia
     Obverse: CAFÉ DE COSTA RICA, Dot
     Reverse: CRISANTO BENEVIDES H, Denomination 1, Dot
     Size: 26 mm
     Metal: Brass

CCR 29   CVGZ, Carmelina Viuda Gonzalez Zamora
    Location: Santo Domingo, Heredia
    Obverse: Café de Costa Rica
    Reverse: Initials CvGZ
    Size: 21.9 mm
    Metal: Brass

CCR 30   DHV, Daniel Hernández Valerio
    Location: San Rafael, Heredia
    Obverse: CAFÉ DE COSTA RICA, Initials DHV, Dot
    Reverse: Ferretería EL IRIS, Denomination 1, Dot
    Size: 25 mm
    Metal: Brass

CCR 31   DHV, Daniel Hernández Valerio Error DVH Underneath
    Location: San Rafael, Heredia
    Obverse: CAFÉ DE COSTA RICA, Initials DHV, Dot
    Reverse: Ferretería EL IRIS, Denomination 1, Dot
    Size: 25 mm
    Metal: Brass

CCR 32   Dora Zamora Chaves
    Location: Santo Domingo, Heredia
    Obverse: CAFÉ DE COSTA RICA, Denomination 1
    Reverse: DORA ZAMORA CH HEREDIA
    Size: 25.8 mm
    Metal: Brass

CCR 33   DR
    Location:
    Obverse: Café de Costa Rica, Initials DR
    Reverse: Blank
    Size: 17.9 mm
    Metal: Zinc Coated

CCR 34   E
    Location:
    Obverse: CAFÉ DE COSTA RICA, Denomination ½
    Reverse: Initial E
    Size: 22.7 mm
    Metal: Brass

CCR 35   E
        Location:
        Obverse: CAFÉ DE COSTA RICA, Denomination 1
        Reverse: Initial E
        Size: 27 mm
        Metal: Brass

CCR 36   ERC, Enrique Rodríguez Castro
        Location: Alajuela
        Obverse: CAFÉ DE COSTA RICA, Denomination 1
        Reverse: Initials ERC
        Size: 27 MM
        Metal: Brass

 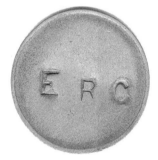

CCR 37   ES
        Location:
        Obverse: CAFÉ DE COSTA RICA, Denomination 1
        Reverse: Initials ES
        Size: 27 mm
        Metal: Brass

CCR 38   EV, Edgar Vargas
    Location: San Pedro de Poás, Alajuela
    Obverse: CAFÉ DE COSTA RICA, Dot
    Reverse: Initials EV, Denomination 1
    Size: 25.8 mm
    Metal: Brass

CCR 39   EVC, Evangelina Valerio C.
    Location: Heredia
    Obverse: Café de Costa Rica, Initials EVC
    Reverse: Blank
    Size: 24 mm
    Metal: Zinc Coated

CCR 40   FACM, Francisco y Alvaro Collado Montealegre
    Location:
    Obverse: CAFÉ DE COSTA RICA, Denomination 5
    Reverse: Initials FACM
    Size: 31.7 mm
    Metal: Brass

CCR 41   FCO ORLI, Francisco José Orlich, Former President of Costa Rica
    Location:
    Obverse: CAFÉ DE COSTA RICA, Denomination 1
    Reverse: Initials FCO ORLI, X's overtop old initials JV
    Size: 27 mm
    Metal: Brass

CCR 42   Ferretería EL IRIS, Basic Design
    Location:
    Obverse: CAFÉ DE COSTA RICA, Dot
    Reverse: Ferretería EL IRIS, Denomination ½, Dot
    Size: 23 mm
    Metal: Brass

CCR 43   Ferretería El IRIS, Heart
    Location:
    Obverse: CAFÉ DE COSTA RICA
    Reverse: Ferretería EL IRIS, Denomination 1, Heart, Dot
    Size: 25 mm
    Metal: Brass

CCR 44   FPR
    Location:
    Obverse: Café de Costa Rica, Initials FPR
    Reverse: Blank
    Size: Octagonal 24 mm
    Metal: Zinc Coated

CCR 45   GBE, German Benevides Esquivel, son of Crisanto Benevides
    Location: Heredia
    Obverse: CAFÉ DE COSTA RICA, Engraved GBE, Dot
    Reverse: CRISANTO BENEVIDES, Denomination 1, Dot
    Size: 21.9 mm
    Metal: Brass

CCR 46   GG
    Location:
    Obverse: Café de Costa Rica, Initials GG
    Reverse: Denomination 1.00
    Size: 21.9 mm
    Metal: Brass

CCR 47   GM, Gonzalo Irola Madrigal
   Location: Paraíso, Cartago
   Obverse: Café de Costa Rica, Initials GM and GI
   Reverse: Blank
   Size: 24 mm
   Metal: Zinc Coated

CCR 48   GRQ, Gilberto Rivera Q
   Location: San Rafael, Poás, Alajuela
   Obverse: CAFÉ DE COSTA RICA, Denomination ¼
   Reverse: Initials GRQ
   Size: 19 mm
   Metal: Brass

CCR 49   GRQ, Gilberto Rivera Q
   Location: San Rafael, Poás, Alajuela
   Obverse: CAFÉ DE COSTA RICA, Denomination 1
   Reverse: Initials GRQ
   Size: 27 mm
   Metal: Brass

CCR 50   IGG, Isaías Gomez Gomez (Father)
    Location: Heredia
    Obverse: CAFÉ DE COSTA RICA, Initials IGG, Dot
    Reverse: Ferretería EL IRIS, Denomination ¼, Dot
    Size: 21.1 mm
    Metal: Brass

CCR 51   IH, Isidro Hernández
    Location:
    Obverse: Café de Costa Rica, Initials IH
    Reverse: Blank
    Size: 21.9 mm
    Metal: Brass

CCR 52   INVU, Instituto Nacional de Vivienda Urbana
    Location: San José
    Obverse: CAFÉ DE COSTA RICA, Denomination ¼
    Reverse: Initials INVU
    Size: 19 mm
    Metal: Brass

CCR 53   INVU, Instituto Nacional de Vivienda Urbana
    Location: San José
    Obverse: CAFÉ DE COSTA RICA, Denomination ½
    Reverse: Initials INVU
    Size: 22.7 mm
    Metal: Brass

CCR 54   INVU, Instituto Nacional de Vivienda Urbana
    Location: San José
    Obverse: CAFÉ DE COSTA RICA, Initials INVU, Dot
    Reverse: Ferretería EL IRIS, Denomination ½, Dot
    Size: 23 mm
    Metal: Brass

CCR 55   ITCO, Instituto de Tierras y Colonización
    Location: San José
    Obverse: CAFÉ DE COSTA RICA, Denomination 1
    Reverse: Initials ITCO in a triangle
    Size: 27 mm
    Metal: Brass

CCR 56   J, MCH
    Location: San Rafael, Heredia
    Obverse: Café de Costa Rica, Initial J
    Reverse: Initials MCH, Manuel Camacho Hernández
    Size: 21.9 mm
    Metal: Brass

CCR 57   JA, Julio Arias
    Location: Santo Domingo, Heredia
    Obverse: CAFÉ DE COSTA RICA, Denomination ½
    Reverse: Initials JA
    Size: 22.7 mm
    Metal: Brass

CCR 58   JB, Joaquín Benavides
    Location: Santo Domingo, Heredia
    Obverse: CAFÉ DE COSTA RICA, Denomination ½
    Reverse: Initials JB
    Size: 22.7 mm
    Metal: Brass

CCR 59   Juan Bautista Mena
    Location: San Antonio de Belén, Heredia
    Obverse: CAFÉ DE COSTA RICA, J.B. MENA
    Reverse: Denomination 30
    Size: 24 mm
    Metal: Brass

CCR 60   Juan Bautista Mena
    Location: San Antonio de Belén, Heredia
    Obverse: CAFÉ DE COSTA RICA, J.B. MENA
    Reverse: Denomination 40
    Size: 24 mm
    Metal: Brass

CCR 61   Juan Bautista Mena
    Location: San Antonio de Belén, Heredia
    Obverse: CAFÉ DE COSTA RICA, J.B. MENA
    Reverse: Denomination 50
    Size: 24 mm
    Metal: Brass

CCR 62   JC, José Cubero
    Location: Guadalupe
    Obverse: Café de Costa Rica, Initials JC
    Reverse: Blank
    Size: 17.9 mm
    Metal: Zinc Coated

CCR 63   JH, Juan Hernández
    Location: San Rafael, Heredia
    Obverse: Café de Costa Rica, Initials JH
    Reverse: Blank
    Size: 21.9 mm
    Metal: Brass

CCR 64   JJ
    Location:
    Obverse: Café de Costa Rica, Denomination 15, Holed
    Reverse: Initials JJ S, Holed
    Size: 21.9 mm
    Metal: Zinc Coated

CCR 65   JL
   Location:
   Obverse: Café de Costa Rica
   Reverse: Initials JL
   Size: 17.9 mm
   Metal: Zinc Coated

CCR 66   JLC, Joaquín Luna Cerdas
   Location:
   Obverse: CAFÉ DE COSTA RICA, Initials JLC, Dot
   Reverse: Denomination ½
   Size: 23.7 mm
   Metal: Brass

CCR 67   J.L.V., Juan León Villalobos
   Location: San Pablo, Heredia
   Obverse: CAFÉ DE COSTA RICA, Initials J.L.V., Dot
   Reverse: Denomination ¼
   Size: 22.2 mm
   Metal: Brass

CCR 68   J.L.V., Juan León Villalobos
    Location: San Pablo, Heredia
    Obverse: CAFÉ DE COSTA RICA, Initials J.L.V., Dot
    Reverse: Denomination ½
    Size: 24.1 mm
    Metal: Brass

CCR 69   J.L.V., Juan León Villalobos
    Location: San Pablo, Heredia
    Obverse: CAFÉ DE COSTA RICA, Initials J.L.V., Dot
    Reverse: Denomination 1
    Size: 25.7 mm
    Metal: Brass

CCR 70   JLV, Juan León Villalobos
    Location: San Pablo, Heredia
    Obverse: Café de Costa Rica, Initials JLV
    Reverse: Blank
    Size: 21.9 mm
    Metal: Brass

CCR 71   JLV, Juan León Villalobos
    Location: San Pablo, Heredia
    Obverse: CAFÉ DE COSTA RICA, Initials JLV, Dot
    Reverse: Denomination ½
    Size: 24 mm
    Metal: Brass

CCR 72   JN
    Location:
    Obverse: CAFÉ DE COSTA RICA, Denomination ½
    Reverse: Initials JN
    Size: 22.7 mm
    Metal: Brass

CCR 73   JPZ, José Procopio Zamora
    Location: Santo Tomás, Santo Domingo, Heredia
    Obverse: Café de Costa Rica, Initials JPZ
    Reverse: Ampersand
    Size: 24 mm
    Metal: Zinc Coated

CCR 74   JR, Finca de Don Pedro Díaz Granadilla
  Location:
  Obverse: Café de Costa Rica, Allegorical Symbol
  Reverse: Initials JR
  Size: 21.9 mm
  Metal: Brass

CCR 75   JSL, Julio Sánchez Lepiz
  Location: Heredia
  Obverse: Café de Costa Rica, Initials JSL
  Reverse: Blank
  Size: 24 mm
  Metal: Zinc Coated

CCR 76   JSL, Julio Sánchez Lepiz
  Location: Heredia
  Obverse: Café de Costa Rica, Initials JSL
  Reverse: Blank
  Size: 21.9 mm
  Metal: Brass

CCR 77   JSL, Julio Sánchez Lepiz
    Location: Heredia
    Obverse: Café de Costa Rica, Initials JSL
    Reverse: Initials CC
    Size: 21.9 mm
    Metal: Brass

CCR 78   JV, Juan Vásquez
    Location: Las Cañas, Alajuela
    Obverse: CAFÉ DE COSTA RICA, Denomination ¼
    Reverse: Initials JV
    Size: 19 mm
    Metal: Brass

CCR 79   JV, Juan Vásquez
    Location: Las Cañas, Alajuela
    Obverse: CAFÉ DE COSTA RICA, Denomination 1
    Reverse: Initials JV
    Size: 27 mm
    Metal: Brass

CCR 80   JV, Juan Vásquez
    Location: Las Cañas, Alajuela
    Obverse: CAFÉ DE COSTA RICA, Dot
    Reverse: Initials JV, Denomination 1
    Size: 27 mm
    Metal: Brass

CCR 81   La Guaria, Alfredo Montealegre
    Location: Heredia
    Obverse: CAFÉ DE COSTA RICA, Denomination ¼
    Reverse: Initials LA GUARIA
    Size: 19 mm
    Metal: Brass

CCR 82   Hacienda La Isabel, Compañía Cafetalera La Isabel
    Location: Turrialba, Cartago
    Obverse: Café de Costa Rica, Stamped 6 Point Flower, Initial O
    Reverse: Stamped 6 Point Flower
    Size: 24 mm
    Metal: Zinc Coated

CCR 83   LF, Luis Fernández
    Location: Paraíso, Cartago
    Obverse: Café de Costa Rica, Initials LF
    Reverse: Initial I
    Size: 21.9 mm
    Metal: Brass

CCR 84   LJC, Luis Javier Guier
    Location: Cartago
    Obverse: Café de Costa Rica, Initials LJG
    Reverse: Denomination ¼
    Size: 17.9 mm
    Metal: Zinc Coated

CCR 85   LJC, Luis Javier Guier
    Location: Cartago
    Obverse: Café de Costa Rica, Initials LJG
    Reverse: Denomination ½
    Size: 21.9 mm
    Metal: Brass

CCR 86   LR, Lola Rodríguez Pérez
    Location: Heredia
    Obverse: Café de Costa Rica, Initials LR
    Reverse: Blank
    Size: 21.9 mm
    Metal: Brass

CCR 87   LSM
    Location:
    Obverse: Café de Costa Rica
    Reverse: Initials LSM
    Size: 24 mm
    Metal: Zinc Coated

CCR 88   LSM
    Location:
    Obverse: Café de Costa Rica
    Reverse: Initials LSM
    Size: 21.9 mm
    Metal: Brass

CCR 89   M, Samuel Arias
    Location: San Francisco, Heredia
    Obverse: CAFÉ DE COSTA RICA, Initial M, Denomination ¼
    Reverse: Initials MVJ
    Size: 19 mm
    Metal: Brass

CCR 90   MAM, Mario Alvarado Morera
    Location: San Rafael, Poás, Alajuela
    Obverse: CAFÉ DE COSTA RICA, Denomination ¼
    Reverse: Initials MAM
    Size: 19 mm
    Metal: Brass

CCR 91   MAM, Mario Alvarado Morera
    Location: San Rafael, Poás, Alajuela
    Obverse: CAFÉ DE COSTA RICA, Denomination ½
    Reverse: Initials MAM
    Size: 22.7 mm
    Metal: Brass

CCR 92   MAM, Mario Alvarado Morera
    Location: San Rafael, Poás, Alajuela
    Obverse: CAFÉ DE COSTA RICA, Denomination 1
    Reverse: Initials MAM
    Size: 27 mm
    Metal: Brass

CCR 93   MCH, Manuel Camacho Hernández, see CCR 56
    Location: San Rafael, Heredia
    Obverse: Café de Costa Rica, Initials MCH
    Reverse: Blank
    Size: 21.9 mm
    Metal: Brass

CCR 94   MP, Miguel Pérez
    Location: Heredia
    Obverse: CAFÉ DE COSTA RICA, Denomination ¼
    Reverse: Initials MP
    Size: 19 mm
    Metal: Brass

CCR 95   MP, Miguel Pérez
    Location: Heredia
    Obverse: CAFÉ DE COSTA RICA, Denomination 1
    Reverse: Initials MP
    Size: 27 mm
    Metal: Brass

CCR 96   MSF
    Location:
    Obverse: CAFÉ DE COSTA RICA, Denomination 1
    Reverse: Initials MSF
    Size: 27 mm
    Metal: Brass

CCR 97   MT, Miguel Trejos
    Location:
    Obverse: Café de Costa Rica, Initials MT
    Reverse: Blank
    Size: 17.9 mm
    Metal: Zinc Coated

CCR 98   MT, Miguel Trejos
   Location:
   Obverse: Café de Costa Rica, Initials MT
   Reverse: Blank
   Size: 24 mm
   Metal: Zinc Coated

CCR 99   MVB
   Location:
   Obverse: CAFÉ DE COSTA RICA, Denomination 1
   Reverse: Initials MVB
   Size: 27 mm
   Metal: Brass

CCR 100   NM
   Location:
   Obverse: Café de Costa Rica, Initials NM
   Reverse: Blank
   Size: 24 mm
   Metal: Zinc Coated

CCR 101   OC, Octavio Campos
    Location: Palmares, Alajuela
    Obverse: Café de Costa Rica, Denomination 25
    Reverse: Initials OC
    Size: 24 mm
    Metal: Zinc Coated

CCR 102   OC FJQ
    Location:
    Obverse: Café de Costa Rica, Denomination 25
    Reverse: Initials OC Horizontally, Initials FJQ Vertically
    Size: 24 mm
    Metal: Zinc Coated

CCR 103   OP, Oscar Pacheco Ortiz
    Location: San Pablo de Barva, Heredia
    Obverse: Café de Costa Rica
    Reverse: Initials OP
    Size: 24 mm
    Metal: Zinc Coated

CCR 104   P, Joaquín Picado Saenz
    Location: Paraíso, Cartago
    Obverse: Café de Costa Rica, Initial P
    Reverse: Blank
    Size: 17.9 mm
    Metal: Zinc Coated

CCR 105   PP
    Location:
    Obverse: Café de Costa Rica, Initials PP
    Reverse: Blank
    Size: 21.9 mm
    Metal: Brass

CCR 106   PP JU, Joaquín Ugalde, see Café 7
    Location: San Joaquín de Flores, Heredia
    Obverse: Café de Costa Rica, Initials PP
    Reverse: Initials JU
    Size: 21.9 mm
    Metal: Brass

CCR 107   RGB, Raúl Gonzalez Badilla
    Location: Santa Ana
    Obverse: CAFÉ DE COSTA RICA, Denomination 1
    Reverse: Initials RGB
    Size: 27 mm
    Metal: Brass

CCR 108   Sanchez Cortes Hermanos
    Location: Heredia
    Obverse: CAFÉ DE COSTA RICA, Denomination ¼
    Reverse: Initials SC HNOS
    Size: 19 mm
    Metal: Brass

CCR 109   Sanchez Cortes Hermanos
    Location: Heredia
    Obverse: CAFÉ DE COSTA RICA, Denomination 1
    Reverse: Initials SC HNOS
    Size: 27 mm
    Metal: Brass

CCR 110   SL, Siquiares
   Location: Turrialba
   Obverse: CAFÉ DE COSTA RICA, Denomination ¼
   Reverse: Initials SL
   Size: 19 mm
   Metal: Brass

CCR 111   SL, Siquiares
   Location: Turrialba
   Obverse: CAFÉ DE COSTA RICA, Denomination ½
   Reverse: Initials SL
   Size: 22.7 mm
   Metal: Brass

CCR 112   TOTO, Carlos Rodríguez
   Location: Palmares
   Obverse: Café de Costa Rica, Initials TOTO
   Reverse: Blank
   Size: 24 mm
   Metal: Zinc Coated

CCR 113   Three Diamonds
Location:
Obverse: Café de Costa Rica, Three Diamonds
Reverse: Initials GU
Size: 21.9 mm
Metal: Brass

CCR 114   TV
Location:
Obverse: Café de Costa Rica, Initials TV
Reverse: Denomination 1
Size: 21.9 mm
Metal: Brass

CCR 115   UBR, Uriel Badilla Rojas
Location: Alajuelita, San José
Obverse: Café de Costa Rica, Initials UBR
Reverse: Blank
Size: 21.9 mm
Metal: Brass

Cafe de Costa Rica Aluminum

I separated these tokens because they are aluminum, and there are few of these.

AL 1   Basic Design
    Location:
    Obverse: CAFÉ DE COSTA RICA, Denomination ¼
    Reverse: Blank
    Size: 19 mm
    Metal: Aluminum

AL 2   B
    Location:
    Obverse: CAFÉ
    Reverse: B, Initial K
    Size: 19.4 mm
    Metal: Aluminum

AL 3 BSR, Beneficio San Rafael, see CCR 18
  Location: Puriscal
  Obverse: CAFÉ DE COSTA RICA, Denomination 1
  Reverse: Initials BSR
  Size: 27.1 mm
  Metal: Aluminum

AL 4 CTL SM, Cafetalera Turnon Limitada San Miguel
  Location: San Miguel
  Obverse: CAFÉ DE COSTA RICA, Denomination 1
  Reverse: Initials CTLSM
  Size: 27.1 mm
  Metal: Aluminum

AL 5 E, Carlos Salazar Chacon
  Location: Heredia
  Obverse: CAFE
  Reverse: E
  Size: 19.4 mm
  Metal: Aluminum

AL 6   EVV, Evelio Villalobos Villalobos
        Location:
        Obverse: CAFÉ DE COSTA RICA, Denomination ½
        Reverse: Initials EVV
        Size: 23 mm
        Metal: Aluminum

AL 7   FLM
        Location: Tambor de Alajuela
        Obverse: CAFÉ DE COSTA RICA, Denomination ½
        Reverse: Initials FLM
        Size: 23 mm
        Metal: Aluminum

AL 8   HRV, Hacienda Vargas
        Location: Heredia
        Obverse: CAFÉ DE COSTA RICA, Denomination 1
        Reverse: Initials HRV
        Size: 27.1 mm
        Metal: Aluminum

AL 9 I
  Location:
  Obverse: CAFÉ
  Reverse: I
  Size: 19.9 mm
  Metal: Aluminum

AL 10 Juan María Solera Rodríguez
  Location: Heredia
  Obverse: CAFÉ, Flowers above and below CAFE
  Reverse: Initials J.M.S.R., Flowers above and below initials
  Size: 19 mm
  Metal: Aluminum

AL 11 Juan María Solera Rodríguez
  Location: Heredia
  Obverse: CAFÉ, Symbols above and below CAFE
  Reverse: Initials J.M.S.R., Symbols above and below initials
  Size: 24.4 mm
  Metal: Aluminum

AL 12   LP
    Location:
    Obverse: CAFÉ DE COSTA RICA, Denomination 1
    Reverse: Initials LP
    Size: 27.1 mm
    Metal: Aluminum

AL 13   MA, Mario Alvarado Morera
    Location: San Rafael, Poás Alajuela
    Obverse: CAFÉ DE COSTA RICA, Denomination 1
    Reverse: Initials MA
    Size: 27.1 mm
    Metal: Aluminum

AL 14   MC, Mario Castro
    Location: Cinco Esquinas, Tibas
    Obverse: CAFÉ DE COSTA RICA, Denomination ¼
    Reverse: Initials MC
    Size: 19 mm
    Metal: Aluminum

AL 15   MM, Mario Alvarado Morera, see AL 13
    Location: San Rafael, Poás, Alajuela
    Obverse: CAFÉ DE COSTA RICA, Denomination 1
    Reverse: Initials MM
    Size: 27.1 mm
    Metal: Aluminum

AL 16   OEF
    Location:
    Obverse: CAFÉ DE COSTA RICA, Denomination 1, Initial R
    Reverse: Initials Vertically OEF
    Size: 27.1 mm
    Metal: Aluminum

AL 17   OR
    Location:
    Obverse: CAFÉ DE COSTA RICA, Denomination ½, Initial R
    Reverse: Initial O
    Size: 23 mm
    Metal: Aluminum

AL 18   P JMB, José Meléndez B
    Location: San Sebastián
    Obverse: CAFE
    Reverse: P, Initials JMB
    Size: 19.4 mm
    Metal: Aluminum

Café

This is a small collection of stock Café tokens. They may have been used as counters.

CAFE 1   A Carlos Salazar Chacon
    Location: Heredia
    Obverse: CAFE
    Reverse: A
    Size: 19.7 mm
    Metal: Brass

CAFE 2   CB
    Location:
    Obverse: CAFÉ, Initials CB
    Reverse: UNA
    Size: 19.2 mm
    Metal: Brass

CAFE 3   E large
    Location:
    Obverse CAFÉ
    Reverse: Large E
    Size: 19.4 mm
    Metal: Brass

CAFE 4   E small, PGG
    Location:
    Obverse: CAFÉ, Initials PGG
    Reverse: Small E
    Size: 19.8 mm
    Metal: Brass

CAFE 5   H, A
    Location:
    Obverse: CAFÉ, Initial A
    Reverse: H, Initial A
    Size: 19.4 mm
    Metal: Brass

CAFE 6   Francisco Bolandi
    Location: Montes de Oca, San José
    Obverse: CAFÉ, Initial 7
    Reverse: F. BOLANDI, Initials ELISA, Dot
    Size: 19.9 mm
    Metal Brass

CAFE 7   JU, Joaquín Ugalde
    Location: San Joaquín de Flores, Heredia
    Obverse: CAFÉ, Initials 18
    Reverse: Initials JU
    Size: 23.2 mm
    Metal: Brass

CAFE 8   JU, Joaquín Ugalde
    Location: San Joaquín de Flores, Heredia
    Obverse: CAFÉ, Initials 18
    Reverse: Initials JU, Initials 88
    Size: 23.2 mm
    Metal: Brass

CAFE 9   JU, Joaquín Ugalde and Bidal Rodríguez
    Location: San Joaquín de Flores
    Obverse: CAFÉ, Initials 18
    Reverse: Initials JU, Initials BR vertically
    Size: 23.2 mm
    Metal: Brass

CAFE 10   KK
    Location:
    Obverse: CAFÉ, Initial K
    Reverse: Initials KK
    Size: 23.2 mm
    Metal: Brass

CAFE 11   M, JRZ
    Location:
    Obverse: CAFÉ, Initials JRZ
    Reverse: M
    Size: 19.4 mm
    Metal: Brass

CAFE 12 O, JRZ
    Location:
    Obverse: CAFÉ, Initials JRZ
    Reverse: O
    Size: 19.4 mm
    Metal: Brass

CAFE 13 OP, Oscar Pacheco Ortiz, see CCR 103
    Location: San Pablo de Barva, Heredia
    Obverse: CAFÉ, Initials OP
    Reverse: Initials OP
    Size: 19.2 mm
    Metal: Brass

CAFE 14 P, Joaquín Picado Sáenz, see CCR 104
    Location: Paraíso, Cartago
    Obverse: CAFE
    Reverse: Initials 36 and P Facing Down
    Size: 19.2 mm
    Metal: Brass

CAFE 15   P, Joaquín Picado Sáenz, see CCR 104
    Location: Paraíso, Cartago
    Obverse: CAFÉ
    Reverse: Initials 36 and P Upside Down
    Size: 19.2 mm
    Metal: Brass

CAFE 16   P
    Location:
    Obverse: CAFÉ
    Reverse: P
    Size: 19.4 mm
    Metal: Brass

CAFE 17   PA CH
    Location:
    Obverse: CAFÉ, Initials PA
    Reverse: Initials CH 36
    Size: 23.2 mm
    Metal: Brass

CAFE 18   P CH
    Location:
    Obverse: CAFÉ, Initial P, Initials CH
    Reverse: UNA Initials 36, Initials PA
    Size: 23.2 mm
    Metal: Brass

CAFE 19   Q
    Location:
    Obverse: CAFÉ
    Reverse: Q, Initials BE
    Size: 19.4 mm
    Metal: Brass

Café de Costa Rica Almacén Gamboa

This is the second largest set of stock coffee tokens. One thing that is apparent throughout is that there are dots on the bottom of both faces. The dots are in two sizes—large and small.

AG 1.   AB
     Location:
     Obverse: CAFÉ DE COSTA RICA, Initials AB, Dot
     Reverse: ALMACEN GAMBOA, Denomination ½, Dot
     Size: 23 mm
     Metal: Brass

AG 2.   AB
     Location:
     Obverse: CAFÉ DE COSTA RICA, Initials AB, Dot
     Reverse: ALMACEN GAMBOA, Denomination 1, Dot
     Size: 25 mm
     Metal: Brass

AG 3.   AG
    Location:
    Obverse: CAFÉ DE COSTA RICA, Initials AG, Dot
    Reverse: ALMACEN GAMBOA, Denomination ½, Dot
    Size: 23 mm
    Metal: Brass

AG 4.   AGA, Adelo García Alvarado
    Location: Santo Domingo, Heredia
    Obverse: CAFÉ DE COSTA RICA, Initials AGA, Dot
    Reverse: ALMACEN GAMBOA, Denomination 1, Dot
    Size: 25 mm
    Metal: Brass

AG 5.   Anchors
    Location:
    Obverse: CAFÉ DE COSTA RICA, Dot, Anchors
    Reverse: ALMACEN GAMBOA, Denomination 1, Dot, Anchor
    Size: 25 mm
    Metal: Brass

AG 6.   AO
   Location:
   Obverse: CAFÉ DE COSTA RICA, Dot, Initials AO
   Reverse: ALMACEN GAMBOA, Denomination 1, Dot
   Size: 25 mm
   Metal: Brass

AG 7.   ARP, Adela Rodríguez Pérez
   Location: Heredia
   Obverse: CAFÉ DE COSTA RICA, Initials ARP, Dot
   Reverse: ALMACEN GAMBOA, Denomination 1, Dot
   Size: 25 mm
   Metal: Brass

AG 8.   AV, Aurelia Villalobos
   Location: Santo Domingo, Heredia
   Obverse: CAFÉ DE COSTA RICA, Initials AV, Dot
   Reverse: ALMACEN GAMBOA, Denomination 1, Dot
   Size: 25 mm
   Metal: Brass

AG 9.   AVJ
   Location:
   Obverse: CAFÉ DE COSTA RICA, Initials AVJ, Dot
   Reverse: ALMACEN GAMBOA, Denomination 1, Dot
   Size: 25 mm
   Metal: Brass

AG 10.   AVZ, Araceli Villalobos Zamora
   Location: Santo Domingo, Heredia
   Obverse: CAFÉ DE COSTA RICA, Initials AVZ, Dot
   Reverse: ALMACEN GAMBOA, Denomination ¼, Dot
   Size: 21.1 mm
   Metal: Brass

AG 11.   AVZ, Araceli Villalobos Zamora
   Location: Santo Domingo, Heredia
   Obverse: CAFÉ DE COSTA RICA, Initials AVZ, Dot
   Reverse: ALMACEN GAMBOA, Denomination ½, Dot
   Size: 23 mm
   Metal: Brass

AG 12.   AVZ, Araceli Villalobos Zamora
   Location: Santo Domingo, Heredia
   Obverse: CAFÉ DE COSTA RICA, Initials AVZ, Dot
   Reverse: ALMACEN GAMBOA, Denomination 1, Dot
   Size: 25 mm
   Metal: Brass

AG 13.   Basic Design
   Location:
   Obverse: CAFÉ DE COSTA RICA, Dot
   Reverse: ALMACEN GAMBOA, Denomination ½, Dot
   Size: 23 mm
   Metal: Brass

AG 14.   Basic Design
   Location:
   Obverse: CAFÉ DE COSTA RICA, Dot
   Reverse: ALMACEN GAMBOA, Denomination 1, Dot
   Size: 25 mm
   Metal: Brass

AG 15.   BV
   Location:
   Obverse: CAFÉ DE COSTA RICA, Initials BV, Dot
   Reverse: ALMACEN GAMBOA, Denomination ½, Dot
   Size: 23 mm
   Metal: Brass

AG 16.   BV
   Location:
   Obverse: CAFÉ DE COSTA RICA, Initials BV, Dot
   Reverse: ALMACEN GAMBOA, Denomination 1, Dot
   Size: 25 mm
   Metal: Brass

AG 17.   BVB, Benigno Viquez Barrantes, See CCR 20
   Location: Getsemaní, San Rafael, Heredia
   Obverse: CAFÉ DE COSTA RICA, Initials BVB, Dot
   Reverse: ALMACEN GAMBOA, Denomination 1, Dot
   Size: 25 mm
   Metal: Brass

AG 18.   CC, Carlos Cordero
   Location: Alajuela
   Obverse: CAFÉ DE COSTA RICA, Initials CC, Dot
   Reverse: ALMACEN GAMBOA, Denomination ½, Dot
   Size: 23 mm
   Metal: Brass

AG 19.   Coffee Grinders
   Location:
   Obverse: CAFÉ DE COSTA RICA, Coffee Grinders, Dot
   Reverse: ALMACEN GAMBOA, Denomination ½, Anchor, Dot
   Size: 23 mm
   Metal: Brass

AG 20.   CR, Cipriano Ramírez
   Location: San Rafael
   Obverse: CAFÉ DE COSTA RICA, Initials CR, Dot
   Reverse: ALMACEN GAMBOA, Denomination ½, Dot
   Size: 23 mm
   Metal: Brass

AG 21.   CR, Cipriano Ramírez
   Location: San Rafael
   Obverse: CAFÉ DE COSTA RICA, Initials CR, Dot
   Reverse: ALMACEN GAMBOA, Denomination 1, Dot
   Size: 25 mm
   Metal: Brass

AG 22.   CS
   Location:
   Obverse: CAFÉ DE COSTA RICA, Initials CS, Dot
   Reverse: ALMACEN GAMBOA, Denomination 1, Dot
   Size: 25 mm
   Metal: Brass

AG 23.   CV, Carlos Villalobos Chacon
   Location: Barrio Los Angeles, Santo Domingo, Heredia
   Obverse: CAFÉ DE COSTA RICA, Initials CV, Dot
   Reverse: ALMACEN GAMBOA, Denomination, 1, Dot
   Size: 25 mm
   Metal: Brass

AG 24.   Diamond Shape, Amado Rosabal
    Location: Heredia
    Obverse: CAFÉ DE COSTA RICA, Diamond Shape, Dot
    Reverse: ALMACEN GAMBOA, Denomination ¼, Dot
    Size: 21.1 mm
    Metal: Brass

AG 25.   DR, JV
    Location:
    Obverse: CAFÉ DE COSTA RICA, Initials DR Vertically, Initials JV Horizontally, Dot
    Reverse: ALMACEN GAMBOA, Denomination 1, Dot
    Size: 25 mm
    Metal: Brass

AG 26.   ECH
    Location:
    Obverse: CAFÉ DE COSTA RICA, Initials ECH, Dot
    Reverse: ALMACEN GAMBOA, Denomination ¼, Dot
    Size: 21.1 mm
    Metal: Brass

AG 27.   ER
    Location:
    Obverse: CAFÉ DE COSTA RICA, Initials ER, Holed, Dot
    Reverse: ALMACEN GAMBOA, Denomination ½, Holed, Dot
    Size: 23 mm
    Metal: Brass

AG 28.   ER
    Location:
    Obverse: CAFÉ DE COSTA RICA, Dot
    Reverse: ALMACEN GAMBOA, Denomination 1, Initials ER, Dot
    Size: 25 mm
    Metal: Brass

AG 29.   EV, Edgar Vargas
    Location: San Pedro de Poás, Alajuela
    Obverse: CAFÉ DE COSTA RICA, Dot
    Reverse: ALMACEN GAMBOA, Denomination 1, Initials EV, Dot
    Size: 25 mm
    Metal: Brass

AG 30.   FRP 84
    Location:
    Obverse: CAFÉ DE COSTA RICA, Initials FRP 84, Dot
    Reverse: ALMACEN GAMBOA, Denomination 1, Dot
    Size: 25 mm
    Metal: Brass

AG 31.   GI, Gonzalo Irola Madrigal, see CCR47
    Location: Paraíso, Cartago
    Obverse: CAFÉ DE COSTA RICA, Initials GI, Dot
    Reverse: ALMACEN GAMBOA, Denomination 1, Dot
    Size: 25 mm
    Metal: Brass

AG 32.   GRQ
    Location:
    Obverse: CAFÉ DE COSTA RICA, Initials GRQ, There is a W underneath the Q, Dot
    Reverse: ALMACEN GAMBOA, Denomination 1, Large 1, Large Dot
    Size: 25.8 mm
    Metal: Brass

AG 33.   H
   Location:
   Obverse: CAFÉ DE COSTA RICA, Initial H, Dot
   Reverse: ALMACEN GAMBOA, Denomination ½, Dot
   Size: 23 mm
   Metal: Brass

AG 34.   HR
   Location:
   Obverse: CAFÉ DE COSTA RICA, Initials HR, Dot
   Reverse: ALMACEN GAMBOA, Denomination 1, Dot
   Size: 25 mm
   Metal: Brass

AG 35.   HT, Tomas Saniers Sánchez, Hacienda Tomas
   Location: Calle Vargas, Alajuela
   Obverse: CAFÉ DE COSTA RICA, Initials HT, Dot
   Reverse: ALMACEN GAMBOA, Denomination 1, Large 1, Large Dot
   Size: 25 mm
   Metal: Brass

AG 36.	HXF With an L Underneath the X, Hernández y Fournier
Location: Grecia
Obverse: CAFÉ DE COSTA RICA, Initials 2, HXF, K0, Dot
Reverse: ALMACEN GAMBOA, Denomination ½, Initial E, Dot
Size: 23 mm
Metal: Brass

AG 37.	HXF With an L Underneath the X, Hernández y Fournier
Location: Grecia
Obverse: CAFÉ DE COSTA RICA, Initials 5Q, HXF, K0, Dot
Reverse: ALMACEN GAMBOA, Denomination 1, Initial E, Dot
Size: 25 mm
Metal: Brass

AG 38.	HXF With an L Underneath the X, Hernández y Fournier
Location: Grecia
Obverse: CAFÉ DE COSTA RICA, Initials HXF, Initials K5QQ
Reverse: ALMACEN GAMBOA, Denomination 1, Initial E
Size: 25 mm
Metal: Brass

AG 39.   IG, Isaías Gómez (Son)
   Location: Heredia
   Obverse: CAFÉ DE COSTA RICA, Initials IG, Dot
   Reverse: ALMACEN GAMBOA, Denomination 1, Large 1, Large Dot
   Size: 25.8 mm
   Metal: Brass

AG 40.   IX, Turnon San Isidro
   Location:
   Obverse: CAFÉ DE COSTA RICA, Initials IX, Dot
   Reverse: ALMACEN GAMBOA, Denomination ½, Dot
   Size: 23 mm
   Metal: Brass

AG 41.   J
   Location:
   Obverse: CAFÉ DE COSTA RICA, Initial J, Dot
   Reverse: ALMACEN GAMBOA, Denomination 1, Dot
   Size: 25 mm
   Metal: Brass

AG 42.   JAS, José Armando Solís Rodríguez
    Location: San Pedro de Póas, Alajuela
    Obverse: CAFÉ DE COSTA RICA, Initials JAS, Dot
    Reverse: ALMACEN GAMBOA, Denomination ¼, Dot
    Size: 21.1 mm
    Metal: Brass

AG 43.   JAS, José Armando Solís Rodríguez
    Location: San Pedro de Póas, Alajuela
    Obverse: CAFÉ DE COSTA RICA, Initials JAS, Dot
    Reverse: ALMACEN GAMBOA, Denomination ½, Dot
    Size: 23 mm
    Metal: Brass

AG 44.   JAV, J. Antonio Vargas Salas
    Location: Santo Domingo, Heredia
    Obverse: CAFÉ DE COSTA RICA, Initials JAV, Dot
    Reverse: ALMACEN GAMBOA, Denomination 1, Dot
    Size: 25 mm
    Metal: Brass

AG 45.   JB
    Location:
    Obverse: CAFÉ DE COSTA RICA, Initials JB, Dot
    Reverse: ALMACEN GAMBOA, Denomination ½, Dot
    Size: 23 mm
    Metal: Brass

AG 46.   JGM
    Location:
    Obverse: CAFÉ DE COSTA RICA, Initials JGM, Dot
    Reverse: ALMACEN GAMBOA, Denomination ¼, Dot
    Size: 21.1 mm
    Metal: Brass

AG 47.   JJGL
    Location:
    Obverse: CAFÉ DE COSTA RICA, Initials JJGL, Dot
    Reverse: ALMACEN GAMBOA, Denomination 1, Large 1, Large Dot
    Size: 25.8 mm
    Metal: Brass

AG 48.   JMR, José María Rodríguez Pérez
   Location: Heredia
   Obverse: CAFÉ DE COSTA RICA, Initials JMR, Dot
   Reverse: ALMACEN GAMBOA, Denomination 1, Dot
   Size: 25 mm
   Metal: Brass

AG 49.   JMS, José Manuel Soto
   Location:
   Obverse: CAFÉ DE COSTA RICA, Initials JMS, Dot
   Reverse: ALMACEN GAMBOA, Denomination ¼, Dot
   Size: 23 mm
   Metal: Brass

AG 50.   JMS, José Manuel Soto
   Location:
   Obverse: CAFÉ DE COSTA RICA, Initials JMS, Dot
   Reverse: ALMACEN GAMBOA, Denomination ½, Dot
   Size: 23 mm
   Metal: Brass

AG 51.   JR, Juanita Rojas and four point symbol, there are 6 round punch marks on the reverse. Each round punch mark is on top of the word GAMBOA
Location: Heredia
Obverse: CAFÉ DE COSTA RICA, Initials JR, Dot
Reverse: ALMACEN GAMBOA, Denomination ¼, Dot
Size: 21.1 mm
Metal: Brass

AG 52.   JR, Juanita Rojas and four point symbol
Location: Heredia
Obverse: CAFÉ DE COSTA RICA, Dot
Reverse: ALMACEN GAMBOA, Denomination 1, Initials JR, Dot
Size: 25 mm
Metal: Brass

AG 53.   JS, Julio Sánchez
Location:
Obverse: CAFÉ DE COSTA RICA, Initials JS, Diamond, Dot
Reverse: ALMACEN GAMBOA, Denomination ¼, Dot
Size: 21.1 mm
Metal: Brass

AG 54.   JS, Julio Sánchez
   Location:
   Obverse: CAFÉ DE COSTA RICA, Initials JS, Diamond, Dot
   Reverse: ALMACEN GAMBOA, Denomination 1, Dot
   Size: 25 mm
   Metal: Brass

AG 55.   JV
   Location:
   Obverse: CAFÉ DE COSTA RICA, Initials JV, Dot
   Reverse: ALMACEN GAMBOA, Denomination ¼, Large Dot
   Size: 21.1 mm
   Metal: Brass

AG 56.   JZ, Juan Zamora
   Location: Santo Domingo, Heredia
   Obverse: CAFÉ DE COSTA RICA, Initials JZ, Dot
   Reverse: ALMACEN GAMBOA, Denomination ¼, Large Dot
   Size: 21.1 mm
   Metal: Brass

AG 57.   Key, Alberto Gonzalez Soto
    Location:
    Obverse: CAFÉ DE COSTA RICA, Key Symbol, Dot
    Reverse: ALMACEN GAMBOA, Denomination ¼, Dot
    Size: 21.1 mm
    Metal: Brass

AG 58.   Key, Alberto Gonzales Soto
    Location:
    Obverse: CAFÉ DE COSTA RICA, Key Symbol, Dot
    Reverse: ALMACEN GAMBOA, Denomination ½, Dot
    Size: 23 mm
    Metal: Brass

AG 59.   LRP, Lola Rodríguez Pérez
    Location: Heredia
    Obverse: CAFÉ DE COSTA RICA, Initials LRP, Dot
    Reverse: ALMACEN GAMBOA, Denomination 1, Dot
    Size: 25 mm
    Metal: Brass

AG 60.   LZ, Luis Zamora
   Location:
   Obverse: ALMACEN GAMBOA, Denomination ¼, Dot
   Reverse: CAFÉ DE COSTA RICA, Initials LZ, Dot
   Size: 21.1 mm
   Metal: Brass

AG 61.   LZ, Luis Zamora
   Location: Santo Domingo, Heredia
   Obverse: CAFÉ DE COSTA RICA, Initials LZ, Dot
   Reverse: ALMACEN GAMBOA, Denomination ½, Dot
   Size: 23 mm
   Metal: Brass

AG 62.   MA, Meliciades Azofeifa
   Location:
   Obverse: CAFÉ DE COSTA RICA, Initials MA, Dot
   Reverse: ALMACEN GAMBOA, Denomination ½, Dot
   Size: 23 mm
   Metal: Brass

AG 63.   MA, Meliciades Azofeifa
Location:
Obverse: CAFÉ DE COSTA RICA, Initials MA, Dot
Reverse: ALMACEN GAMBOA, Denomination 1, Dot
Size: 25 mm
Metal: Brass

AG 64.   MM
Location:
Obverse: CAFÉ DE COSTA RICA, Initials MM
Reverse: ALMACEN GAMBOA, Denomination 1, Initials X X X, Dot
Size: 25 mm
Metal: Brass

AG 65.   MM
Location:
Obverse: CAFÉ DE COSTA RICA, Initial 2, Dot
Reverse: ALMACEN GAMBOA, Denomination 1, Initials MM, Dot
Size: 25 mm
Metal: Brass

AG 66.   MV
   Location:
   Obverse: CAFÉ DE COSTA RICA, Initials MV, Dot
   Reverse: ALMACEN GAMBOA, Denomination ¼, Dot
   Size: 21.1 mm
   Metal: Brass

AG 67.   OA, Orfilio Arguello, Hacienda La Roja
   Location: Santo Domingo, Heredia
   Obverse: CAFÉ DE COSTA RICA, Initials OA, Dot
   Reverse: ALMACEN GAMBOA, Denomination 1, Dot
   Size: 25 mm
   Metal: Brass

AG 68.   Pine Tree
   Location:
   Obverse: CAFÉ DE COSTA RICA, Pine Tree, Dot
   Reverse: ALMACEN GAMBOA, Denomination ½, Dot
   Size: 23 mm
   Metal: Brass

AG 69.   OZ
Location:
Obverse: CAFÉ DE COSTA RICA, Initials OZ, Dot
Reverse: ALMACEN GAMBOA, Denomination ½, Dot
Size: 23 mm
Metal: Brass

AG 70.   RAG
Location:
Obverse: CAFÉ DE COSTA RICA, Initials RAG, Dot
Reverse: ALMACEN GAMBOA, Denomination ½, Dot
Size: 23 mm
Metal: Brass

AG 71.   RBA, Coffee Branch Visible Underneath BA
Location:
Obverse: CAFÉ DE COSTA RICA, Initials RBA, Dot
Reverse: ALMACEN GAMBOA, Denomination 1, Dot
Size: 25 mm
Metal: Brass

AG 72.   RJ, Rogelio Jiménez, Las Trojas
    Location: San Miguel
    Obverse: CAFÉ DE COSTA RICA, Initials RJ, Dot
    Reverse: ALMACEN GAMBOA, Denomination ¼, Dot
    Size: 21.1 mm
    Metal: Brass

AG 73.   RJ, Rogelio Jiménez, Las Trojas
    Location:
    Obverse: CAFÉ DE COSTA RICA, Initials RJ, Dot
    Reverse: ALMACEN GAMBOA, Denomination ½, Dot
    Size: 23 mm
    Metal: Brass

AG 74.   RR GE
    Location:
    Obverse: CAFÉ DE COSTA RICA, Initials RR and GE, Dot
    Reverse: ALMACEN GAMBOA, Denomination 1, Dot
    Size: 25 mm
    Metal: Brass

AG 75.   RRN
   Location:
   Obverse: CAFÉ DE COSTA RICA, Initials RR N, Dot
   Reverse: ALMACEN GAMBOA, Denomination 1, Dot
   Size: 25 mm
   Metal: Brass

AG 76.   Running Man
   Location:
   Obverse: CAFÉ DE COSTA RICA, Symbol Running Man, Dot
   Reverse: ALMACEN GAMBOA, Denomination 1, Dot
   Size: 25 mm
   Metal: Brass

AG 77.   Running Man
   Location:
   Obverse: CAFÉ DE COSTA RICA, Dot
   Reverse: ALMACEN GAMBOA, Denomination 1, Symbol Running Man, Dot
   Size: 25 MM
   Metal: Brass

AG 78.   RV
    Location:
    Obverse: CAFÉ DE COSTA RICA, Initials RV, Dot
    Reverse: ALMACEN GAMBOA, Denomination ¼, Dot
    Size: 21.1 mm
    Metal: Brass

AG 79.   RZ, Roberto Zeledón
    Location:
    Obverse: CAFÉ DE COSTA RICA, Initials RZ, Dot
    Reverse: ALMACEN GAMBOA, Denomination ¼, Dot
    Size: 21.1 mm
    Metal: Brass

AG 80.   SA
    Location:
    Obverse: CAFÉ DE COSTA RICA, Initials SA, Dot
    Reverse: ALMACEN GAMBOA, Denomination ¼, Initial G, Dot
    Size: 21.1 mm
    Metal: Brass

AG 81.   Triangle
Location:
Obverse: CAFÉ DE COSTA RICA, Triangle, Dot
Reverse: ALMACEN GAMBOA, Denomination ¼, Dot
Size: 21.1 mm
Metal: Brass

AG 82.   VB
Location:
Obverse: CAFÉ DE COSTA RICA, Initials VB, Dot
Reverse: ALMACEN GAMBOA, Denomination 1, Dot
Size: 25 mm
Metal: Brass

AG 83.   VHB
Location:
Obverse: CAFÉ DE COSTA RICA, Initials VHB, Dot
Reverse: ALMACEN GAMBOA, Denomination 1, Ampersand, Dot
Size: 25 mm
Metal: Brass

AG 84.   VJB
Location:
Obverse: CAFÉ DE COSTA RICA, Initials VJB, Dot
Reverse: ALMACEN GAMBOA, Denomination 1, Dot
Size: 25.8 mm
Metal: Brass

AG 85.   VS
Location:
Obverse: CAFÉ DE COSTA RICA, Dot
Reverse: ALMACEN GAMBOA, Denomination ¼, Initials VS, Dot
Size: 21.1 mm
Metal: Brass

Glossary of selected words

ALMACEN – General store

BARRIO – Neighborhood

BENEFICIO – Benefit

BOLETO – Token

CAFÉ – Coffee

CAFETELERA – Coffee processing plant

CANASTO – Bushel

COLONIZACION – Colonization

CALLE – Street

COMPAÑIA – Company

DE – From or of

EL – The (masculine tense)

FERRETERIA – Hardware store

FINCA – Coffee plantation or farm

HACIENDA – Large farm not always comprised of coffee

HERMANOS – Brothers

INSTITUTO – Institute

LA – The (feminine tense)

LIMITADA – Limited

MIMBRE – Willow twigs

NACIONAL – National

RECIBIDOR – Receiver

SAN – Saint

SANTO – Saint (masculine tense)

TIERRAS – Lands

UNA – One

URBANA – Urban

VIVIENDA – Home

VIUDA – Widow

Y – And

Printed in the United States
By Bookmasters